The Frog Prince

George Ivanoff
Illustrated by Diane Le Feyer

Once upon a time,
there was a story about a princess.
The princess kissed a frog and it turned
into a prince!

Sarah and Joe went to the library to read the story. As they started to read...

...a fairy appeared!
"I am Fifi the Fairytale Fixit Fairy," she said.
"This story is broken.
Can you help me fix it?"

Fifi waved her wand.

Sarah and Joe fell into the book.

They landed by a pond.

A princess was sitting on a rock, crying.
There was a frog beside her.

“What’s wrong?” Joe asked the princess.
“The frog will not let me kiss him!” she said.

"The princess has to kiss you,"
said Joe to the frog,
"or there won't be a story!"

“If she kisses me,” said the frog,
“I’ll turn into a prince.”

“What is wrong with that?” asked Sarah.

"I like eating flies," said the frog.
"And princes don't eat flies."

“The princess will have to let the prince eat flies,” said Joe.

"Yuck!" said the princess, shaking her head. "Well," said Joe, "you can marry a prince who eats flies, or you can marry a frog."

“Okay, but he can only eat flies when I’m not watching,” said the princess.
The princess kissed the frog.
The frog turned into a handsome prince.

"Thank you for fixing the story," said Fifi.
"Now let's go home."
"No," said Sarah.
"Let's go to a pet shop. I'd like to get a frog!"